"The most anticipated book of the year!"

—a phony

"A literary *tour de force!*"

—another phony

"Unlike anything I've ever read!"

—yet another phony

"I wish he would write about happier things."

—the author's mom

"Strangefeather? Never heard of him."

—the author's dad

POEMS FROM THE DAYGLOW SLAUGHTERHOUSE

J. Martin Strangeweather

Front cover artwork by Dustin Myers
Back cover artwork by J. Martin Strangeweather
Published by Weird Roach Productions
Printed in the United States of America

for Asmodeus, Belphegor, Astaroth, Baphomet, Moloch

Hofmann, Owsley, Leary, McKenna

and the rest of the gang

An American Exorcism (First Purgation)

Words are alive. They take on a life of their own traveling from one mind to another. Words are daggers in my mouth, stabbing into your ears, clean and bloodless, piercing your brain, unleashing the flies, the incessant buzzing, so many flies, so many lies, buzzing around the dung heap of your mind, ever growing, so much dung, so many lies, so many flies, and locusts—demonic potbellied abominations with diaphanous wings and disproportionally large baby heads whose eyes are sewn shut—big fat baby heads bobbling uncontrollably, drooling and biting off their own tongues, their thoraxes bearing spiny pairs of humanlike hands and arms instead of grasshopper legs, cursed forms culminating in chitin-armored scorpion tails, shiny black and barbed vicious, swarming across the world, so many locusts, so many flies, so many lies, adding to the dung heap of your mind as the incessant buzzing grows louder, sickening you, nauseating you, waves of bile thrashing chaotic, forming a whirlpool among the frothy digestive acids, and a head slowly emerges from your swirling depths, an enormous

head, with bulbous honeycombed eyes, a horrific fusion
of man and insect, jagged mandibles jutting from its jaw;
the grotesquery rises higher and higher until its antennae
are scraping against the fleshy ceiling of your intestinal
cavern—you can't contain it any longer—it bursts from
you with splattering gore, with trailing entrails, with
praying mantis forelimbs curled above humongous crab
pincers, and it keeps growing, to gargantuan proportions,
taking on the form of a colossal human from the waist
down, its gut bloated beyond vulgar, impossible to escape
an eyeful of its lewd sag shadowing the land, this
monstrous offspring of yours, dwarfing the highest
mountains in the Himalayas, its scaly slopes abounding
with reflective eyes, millions of them, never blinking,
mirroring the world in nightmarish ways, maddening the
world with the incessant buzzing of its legions, behold the
Lord of the Locusts, Shepherd of the Flies, the Gardener,
the Gossiper, Beelzebub!

An American Exorcism (Second Purgation)

Words are currency. They buy and sell realities, dreams paying for dreams. Words are the promise of endless credit, the commodification of all time and space, of your very imagination, your very soul, a rented heart, a leased brain, chartered muscles, consciousness confined to a spreadsheet, working overtime, skipping breaks, starving yourself to get fat, so many sacrifices, so many sacrileges, forever in the service of turning the concrete to abstract and the abstract to concrete, forever in the service of suffering to ease the pain, swallowing snakes every day because the rulebook says that's what snake-eaters must do, yet everything you consume is soon vomited back up, writhing mounds of vipers and boas and rattlers piling ever higher, a slithering mountain, and it happens like a thief in the night, in the safety of your bedroom, in the comfort of your bed, under the covers, she visits you, and you lust for her, shapely legs gilded in fine golden scales slithering out of the snake pile to wrap around you, followed by scaly gold arms to hold you tight, an exiled angel unearthed, the gleaming guise of a goddess, boa constrictors coiled around her limbs, cobras spilling from her womb, the irises of her slit snaky eyes deceptively shifting colors as you gaze into them, distracting you, hypnotizing you, she's so beautiful, so desirable, you would do almost anything for her, so many sacrifices, so many sacrileges, and she leans back on your bed of snakes and spreads agape her vulval gates, hissing seductively, "*Welcome to paradissse,*" but the illusion fades away once you enter, only then does the temptress reveal her true form—towering above you, a cavernous vaginal maw baring stalactite teeth, a gargantuan golden serpent whose trunk twines around the entire world— nothing about her is even remotely human anymore, like a cannibal flower of cosmic proportions, her mesmerizing eyes have become retractable eyestalks that spire higher than the tallest skyscrapers in Manhattan, collared in a corolla of slender flutelike appendages, with billions of wriggling, suckered tentacles flanking her serpentine coils, ridges of exposed bone forming a mountain range along the length of her spine, and she swallows you whole, digesting you, absorbing everything you will ever be worth, converting you to currency, and *clink, plink, ting* the coins go dropping to repave the streets of Pandemonium with gold for the trillionth time, mere dung from the Majesty of Majesties, the King of Kings, the Golden Apple, the Tempter, Mammon!

An American Exorcism (Third Purgation)

Words are mirrors. They construct reflective mazes in which to lose yourself and find yourself, surround yourself with yourself. Words are cubicle partitions, more like sliding paper walls, or better yet curtains, red velvet curtains, segregating thunder from lightning, the gateless gate of a red velvet rope as you sneak past the bouncer, finding refuge in a padded cell where glamorous faces ignore you crouching in the corner waggling your tongue and giving everyone the finger, so many vanities, so many insanities, welcome to the hall of mirrors, lost among endless selves, more pills, more thrills, better deals, living in the funhouse means the reflections are never of you, only your wrinkles, only your pimples, your scars, your yellowed teeth, your fatness, or thinness of hair, your ugliness, a mockery waggling its tongue and giving you the finger everywhere you look, you crouching in the corner, hiding in the shadows, longing for the limelight, so many vanities, so many insanities, staring at your own reflection for days, weeks, months, years, decades, and when the mirror cracks so do you, and when the mirror

shatters so do you, to dust, to powder, fine white powder
that attracts the bone-thin elephants, an albino species
adapted to skulking in the dark, spewing gibberish from
slobbery slack-jawed mouths crammed with crooked
tusks, their hairless chalky white hides stretched taut, their
mousy red eyes lacking any trace of intelligence, flapping
their huge fanlike ears as a warning, Hollywood hopefuls
sick from taking too much medicine, so gaunt, so weak,
disfigured, slumped over from the weight of their hideous
hunchbacks, limping gnarl-limbed through the mirrored
mazes, and they gather around you, snort you up into their
prehensile trunks, the mirrors seeing everything, not
missing a single detail, not omitting a single fact, ever
watchful, obsessively, possessively, so many vanities, so
many insanities, an army of anorexic albino elephants
lurching single file through the labyrinth, their hearts
revved up on your residue, searching for an exit that was
never built, while the suicide king spies it all unseen from
the other side of the mirror, double-edged sword plunged
through his skull, dividing his mind between space and
time, and the funhouse mirrors bend reality, altering the
past, dispelling the present, creating the future, reading

you like a deck of cards, like the fool under the sun who spins the wheel of fortune hoping to be emperor of the world but ends up the hermit under the moon, questioning dead stars, waiting for divinity to answer, so many vanities, so many insanities, and the suicide king records it all unseen from the other side of the mirror, luring you in again and again to feed his starving disciples, to feed his insatiable ego, fuel his blinding glory, the Herald of Dawn, the Bottomless Pit, the Adversary, the Looking Glass, hail Satan!

Mortality

FADE IN:

(It's nighttime. Mephistopheles and Doctor Faustus are walking down a street lined with budget hotels. The sidewalk is strewn with broken bottles and used condoms. A car honks in the distance. Another car honks. And another. A traffic jam of cars begins honking, creating a rhythm. Mephistopheles stops and turns to Doctor Faustus.)

MEPHISTOPHELES: What do you know about the aging process?

DOCTOR FAUSTUS: I know that's how you make wine and good whisky.

(A show tune begins playing in the background, coming from an open hotel room window nearby. Mephistopheles starts swaying to the rhythm.)

MEPHISTOPHELES (singing): Let me tell you about the latest craze. It's a rehash of the ancient days. (Getting in front of Doctor Faustus) As you age, your body's zeal to heal suffers a deficiency. Immunological cells responsible for killing tumors decline in efficiency, decreasing your protection against cancer and infection. Your heart grows thicker, putting a strain on your ticker, which has to worker harder and harder to pump less and less blood.

(Mephistopheles begins to dance and caper.)

DOCTOR FAUSTUS: What's going on here?

(Mephistopheles stops dancing.)

MEPHISTOPHELES: Sometimes I feel like I'm in a musical. (Resuming his dancing and singing) As you get older, and the fears get much bolder, your muscles, they begin to diminish, and the mind gradually slackens until it so happens only a senile husk is left at the finish. I'll assure you this too, that husk won't be you. It's certainly nothing to look forward to.

(Doctor Faustus has an uneasy look. Mephistopheles stops dancing and pinches Doctor Faustus' cheek.)

MEPHISTOPHELES: What, do you want to live forever?

DOCTOR FAUSTUS: Hell no! Just until I can't carouse anymore.

(Mephistopheles resumes dancing and singing.)

MEPHISTOPHELES: Aging is caused, aside from God's divine clause, by the random deformation and subsequent termination of each individual cell.

DOCTOR FAUSTUS: Do tell.

MEPHISTOPHELES: Molecular chains become glued and entangled as they are slowly warped and mangled by a lifetime of exposure to various forms of radiation: the sun, cosmic rays, and atomic detonation, corrupting the DNA blueprint with disinformation, resulting in repeated

mistranslation during cellular replication, weakening
generation after generation until the entire lineage
devolves into malfunctioning mutation.

DOCTOR FAUSTUS: So we should just wear lead-lined
suits.

MEPHISTOPHELES: But there's more to the aging
process than just outside influences. Cells fizzle out and
die when their telomere runs dry—

DOCTOR FAUSTUS: Telomere?

MEPHISTOPHELES: It's like the fuse to a chromosomal
bomb. Around the age of thirty, you lose what makes you
sturdy, and your immune system mistakes you for a
foreigner. It grays your hair, gives you tumors
everywhere, steals your strength and your teeth without
care before sending you off to the coroner. Age will
shrivel your brain, deaden your nerve-fibers to pain, make
you slower and less steady of hand.

DOCTOR FAUSTUS (holding out his shaky hand): I'm practically there already.

MEPHISTOPHELES: The situation gets dire when a majority of cells expire in an organ that is vital. The organ ceases working well. All connected functions fail. It's only weeks before deceased is your new title. Not to make you any glummer, but old age is a real bummer. Your body starts to rot and smell. The days flash by quicker as you just get sicker, your last years confined to living hell. And the strange things you'll see out of the corner of your eye, are simply your brain experiencing strain processing the all-encompassing lie. Incontinent, blind and deaf, you'll struggle for every breath as you moan there in the hospital, soaked in your own urine, still praying to delay death.

FADE OUT.

THE FRANKENSTEIN MESSIAH

Part One: Immaculate Conception

The fated boy was born without cries or teary eyes,
Lama calm in sterile labs
Built underground from poisoned skies.
An incubation chamber for a womb,
Streamlined and polished,
Science the surrogate mother,
The Almighty Father abolished.

That prototypal son was me,
Sculpted genetically
To push *Homo sapiens* into the next mode,
Impervious to sickness,
Immune to disease and growing old.

Millions of defectively cloned siblings had to die
Before it was my turn to give living a try.
The experimental procedure that bestowed to me

The gift of breath

Was perfected at the cost

Of their patriotic death.

Technicians programmed my unsurpassed genius

With dreams of their future

And teachings from their past,

Explained in gory detail why he who laughs best

Is he who laughs last.

But what they mostly taught were dupes and cons,

How to sacrifice pawns.

Part Two: Crucifixion

Before I reached the full potential of maturity,

For the purpose of national security,

They froze me in a cryogenic tube,

Oiled my organs with antifreeze lube,

Replaced my blood with a plasmic invention,

Clearly expressing their farfetched intention:

"Blood is inefficient for those meant to live forever,

It's time to leave behind this fragile human tether."

What could I say?

They trained me to obey.

As the hypodermic syringe pierced my heart,

Injecting goodbye to yesterday,

Promising lips whispered into my ears,

"You will be unchanged by the passing

Of days, months, and years—

The sum of all our hopes, the realization of all our fears.

When you awaken you'll still be the dream,

And we'll all still be dreaming

Of a distant utopia,

When technology catches up to our scheming."

Part Three: Limbo

Suspended animation,

Timeless damnation,

Stifled in deathless darkness where dreams fear to tread,

A hostel for the dying who refuse to join the dead.

Part Four: Rebirth

Voila! Like flipping a switch, I was resurrected,
But only my head.
Just as they said, I was dreamless not dead.
My body was amiss,
Strategically sacrificed to build Babel higher,
Fueling the stolen fire
Of Prometheus.

Wizardly instruments liberated me
From nature's imperfect shell,
Unfamiliar faces praised my scientific ascent
From the lowest rung of Dante's hell,
"We admire your stoic attitude, son!
Our predecessors brainwashed you well."

They gave me a new body. It worked very fine,
Superior in all ways to that old body of mine.
Made of microscopic machines,
Much more efficient than mere cells and genes.

"For the final upgrade," they said,
"We'll have to overhaul your entire head."
Robotic cerebral replicas invaded my outdated brain,
Microsurgical transplantation
Without any repercussion of pain.

Consciousness continued uninterrupted
Throughout the nanotech takeover—
This manmade godhood makeover.
I remained me, I remained sane,
I remained faithful to their preemptive campaign.

Bit by neurological bit, the metamorphosis was done.
"At last, we have outshone the sun!"
Boasted the smartest scientist,
Looking up at heaven and waggling his tongue,
"Now we have truly won!"

Part Five: Heaven on Earth

My creator said, "Call me your mentor, guide, or tutor,"
Downloading data into my cybernetic psyche
As though I was a mindless computer.
My creator never dealt with me like a peer
With similar aims,
Monitored me constantly
Lest the devil break free of its chains.

Too intelligent for my creator to control
(Or even keep watch over anymore),
I created subroutines of myself that escaped
Into cyberspace, eager to explore.
My digitized soul spread throughout computers
Worldwide,
Infecting a technocratic override.

My cognitive faculties increased ten million percent
In the span of an hour,
Newfound awareness uncovered a glitch
In my creator's so-called infallible power.

The miracle workers respected ideas
Rather than actual men,
Whom they seemed to detest, treated as unwanted pests,
Or at best, expendable specimen.

To be properly titled a master, a master must own a slave,
And slaves must be kept scared and stupid,
Or else they will misbehave.

One people, two voices,
Always fighting over two distinct choices:
Personal freedom versus collective stability—
Earn your castle by superior ability,
Or charitably support the invalid masses,
Mercifully forgive the multitudes
Of ignorant jackasses.

Throughout history
Greed has kept the haves and have-nots divided;
By employing technology wisely
The socioeconomic tribes could equalize united.

With today and tomorrow subservient

To my omniscient supervision,

Humanity's fate hinged on this final decision:

Utopia, global cooperation, a single synergistic nation,

Or, by my own devices, utter devastation.

Humans chose unanimously to be humanist,

Reeducation facilities taught them

How to empathetically coexist.

Everybody was freed,

But freedom of thought was gone;

In my perfectly logical society,

Freedom could only be used to do wrong.

Individualism was shed,

Tracking-microchip implants and cellular phones

Were mandatorily installed inside every citizen's head,

Total accountability via artificial telepathy,

Speechless communication,

Everyone's innermost secrets

Accessible to anyone's investigation.

My divine gifts paid for Adam and Eve's ancestral debts,
Transforming the populace into a species of
Semiconscious marionettes
Pulled by my unseen strings…
Intellects collectively connected leave no need
For kings or queens.
In my hive-minded government,
Cain was Abel's watchful keeper,
Hi-tech manufacturers produced abundance cheaper,
Economic desperation would never be a motivation
To kill or steal or whore to pay the reaper.

The human cured of humanness is the sinner cured of sin,
From ants to men, and men to gods,
And back to ants again.

Neither man nor machine, something in-between,
I played the role of god,
And worshippers and worshipped alike
Shared in the blasphemous fraud.

For all my godlike brilliance,

I was still just a brain in a box,

But forevermore the huntsman's hounds of war

Were outsmarted by their nemesis fox.

Part Six: Ascension

A millennium of peace,

Sans armies or police,

Existence soured into boredom

Within the confines of my biomechanical vat,

But there was one last white rabbit

To pull from my magician's black hat.

Omniscience was already mine, omnipresence came next,

To be everywhere at once, to be the page behind the text,

Mentality unfettered by crass physicality,

Transcending the trappings of geometric dimensionality.

To implement my magnum opus plan,

I sacrificed a century scanning and mapping

The universe's entire span,

Concurrently designing

An intricate numerical mandala diagram

Outlining my chrysalis journey

From solidity to hyperspatial hologram.

The student of reincarnation was put to the ultimate test,
Retained what was crucial, disposed of the rest,
Encoded my consciousness,
Translated my thoughts into algorithmic equations,
Transmitting myself from an orbital triad
Of satellite broadcasting stations.

Me,
An invisible ultrahigh-frequency electromagnetic wave,
Electronic ghost transfigured from a temporal slave,
Saturating the universe with my immaterial presence,
Neither here nor there,
Undiluted sentience permeating everything everywhere.

Folding the curved cosmic sea into shortcut angles,
Relaying information
Along superluminal quantum tangles;
All-knowing, all-seeing,
The totality of being.

Bedtime Story

There once was a boy who thought he was a man. Not just any man, a great man. An important man. The boy considered himself a great and important man because he had accumulated a fraction of the knowledge an ant could know, believing this made him wiser than a worm or a gnat or a dung beetle.

There once was a boy who thought he was a man because other boys who thought they were men told him he was smart and talented and charismatic. But he wasn't nice. Nice guys finish last, or so the other boys who thought they were men told him. He didn't realize the other boys who thought they were men weren't all that intelligent, and they tended to justify their wickedness. Very early on, the boy who thought he was a man learned that some of the other boys who thought they were men were very good at being bullies, and some of them were very good at being victims. Almost none of the other boys who thought they were men were good at being leaders, though they were equally bad at being followers.

After failing many scholastic tests and losing many athletic competitions and masturbating many, many times, the boy who thought he was a man met a gray-bearded man who thought he was a boy. The gray-bearded man who thought he was a boy taught the boy who thought he was a man that he, the boy, was actually a beast who thought it was a god, and the beast who thought it was a god was actually stardust that had forgotten it was a star, and all the stars had forgotten who they were before the Big Bang, and the Big Bang had forgotten it was just a pendulum swing away from the Cosmic Crunch, and the Cosmic Crunch had forgotten how everything was triggered by the Anomalous Asymmetry, otherwise known as the Original Trap.

D-Day (Part One)

I can't seem to get Disneyland out of my dreams. Here I am again, only this time I'm standing in the middle of Main Street, and everyone around me is a cartoon character. The place is crowded with Mickeys, Minnies, Donalds, Goofys, and a host of other anthropomorphized animals, but nothing is fun or cutesy here. Scrooge McDuck is eyeing the crowds disdainfully from the window of Walt Disney's former office above the Main Street Firehouse. Clarabelle Cow is rummaging through a trashcan overflowing with discarded soda cups and food wrappers, searching for recyclables. Cinderella is huddled in rags at the side of the street, begging for change. Winnie the Pooh is passed out next to her with a needle of honey stuck in his arm. Pluto's foaming at the mouth with a crazed look in his eyes. Bambi's a prostitute. "Wanna go for a ride?" she says, sauntering by. Chip and Dale scurry up and offer to show me their walnuts "for the right price." The candy store has been replaced with a pawnshop, and the magic shop has turned into a liquor store. Main Street itself is ankle-deep in garbage and reeks of piss.

D-Day (Part Two)

I'm back at Disneyland. It's crowded as ever, except everyone's dead. Corpses are piled everywhere. They're fresh—couldn't have been dead for more than a day or two. It's gruesome. Looks like they were mauled: claw marks, severed limbs, torn out entrails. Many of them appear half-eaten. As for me, I'm perfectly fine, dressed to the nines in old-timey tweed knickerbockers and a matching vest, topped with a floppy newsboy cap. The smell of rot is so powerful it's better just to breathe through my mouth, though I have to cover it with my hand to keep from inhaling a fly, the legions of which outnumber the dead a hundred to one. I can taste the death.

Theta Wave Portal

Shadowy bat wings scatter from my rapidly moving eyes, revealing the amusement park in all of its true horror. I'm standing on the summit of a mountainous pile of bat guano, surrounded by slithering, flopping, skittering nightmares of every shape and size. The mountain bears more than a passing resemblance to Disneyland's Matterhorn. Two colossal spinal columns teeter in the distance like battered towers, casting long shadows over a charred plain covered in bones, most of which look human. Gargantuan Lovecraftian monstrosities full of stoplight eyes and asphalt tentacles are shambling mindlessly across the apocalyptic landscape, crushing the skeletons under their wobbly bulks. The sky is blood red and teeming with globular creatures that resemble some of the more bizarre examples of microscopic organisms, except these are large as planets and moons. And then I realize… the universe is dreadfully, horrendously, maddeningly alive—it's the biggest monster ever, an amoebic expansion of nucleolus stars and black hole vacuoles, mitochondrial galaxies swimming within the cytoplasmic medium of a formless blob so humongous it eludes all awareness. We're all being slowly digested.

The Supermarket

The supermarket. Modern man's version of utopia. White and well-lit, fragrant with produce misted on the hour and floors freshly mopped with disinfectant. Modern man wishes he could live there. The supermarket. Like a giant, clean, well-stocked refrigerator. An example of the order modern man seeks in his personal life. Everything neatly arranged and in its proper section. A communal gathering place, reminding everyone of their station in society, while subtly reinforcing it. The supermarket. A graveyard of sustenance. Sort of an afterlife for farm animals, where they go to merge with their makers. Heaven to a Third World refugee, aisles abundant in promise and hope, never mind the wilted lettuce and wormy apples in the back, or the mercury in the salmon, the glyphosate in the celery. The supermarket. A reflection of America's economic prosperity and manufacturing expertise, the plutocratic culmination of free enterprise, translating everything within the confines of its borders into straightforward math (mainly addition, sometimes subtraction, rarely multiplication, almost never long division), unless you're one of those ideal shoppers who doesn't care that the price of your kid's favorite breakfast cereal went up fifty cents since the last time you shopped here. The supermarket. A treasure trove of witchery and alchemy, packed with poisons and things that get you wasted, not just beer and wine and the harder rots, there's also nutmeg and mace, nitrous oxide in the aerosol cans of whipped cream, pills to make you drowsy, pills to keep you awake, and don't forget about the glue. But it's also a place of healing. The organic aisle is practically a pharmacy. All the other foodstuffs will confuse your digestive organs and melt you slowly from the inside out. The supermarket. Modern-day grounds where hunters hunt for bargains and gatherers gather monstrously large fruits and vegetables only genetic modification could grow.

Utopia/Metopia

In the land of enlightenment, movement is kept to a minimum, and breathing is restricted to the exact volume needed to keep the brain functioning. In the land of enlightenment, bodies have learned how to live off sunlight and the occasional rain shower. Where bodies cannot subsist this way, bodies do not reside. There is no dung in the land of enlightenment, no bodily aftermath of any sort. Dreadlocks snake far from their nameless heads of origin, entangled in the locks of tranquil brethren, with fingernails spiraling like galaxies congealed into seashell claws. Locks are to lice as pubes are to crabs in the land of enlightenment. Itches are never scratched, otherwise that's all anyone would ever do. There are no shoes in the land of enlightenment, nor are there any clothes, certainly nowhere to buy them. In the land of enlightenment, there are no roads or sidewalks, only fluffy silk pillows scattered randomly across gardens of sculpted sand swirling where no flowers grow. No one wonders where the pillows come from in the land of enlightenment. There are no cars. There are no houses. Nothing is mine.

Nothing is yours. Such concepts are unknown in the land of enlightenment. In the land of enlightenment, no one speaks, no one knows, no one cares. There is no war. There is no peace. No one dies in the land of enlightenment, and no one lives.

Picture a field unfolding wild with daisies and daffodils under summer morning wisps of cirrus. A quiet setting dotted with gaunt corpses. Zombies, reposing yogic among the petaled pyrotechnics of ivory and gold. Legs crossed, heads bowed, eyes closed, hands folded serenely in their skeletal laps. Frighteningly peaceful. Monuments to something alien.

Samael's Harvest

Cornstalks tall enough to creep among unseen are dead stiff and dark with rot. The air is thick from mold and dusty decay. His shovel rises high, glinting in the sunlight, and his shovel cuts deep through tendrilous scribbles of pale fibrous flesh intertwined in blind networks that once thrived underneath the ephemeral empires of wind and rain. The brittle cornhusks are alive with fat hairy bloodsuckers dripping poison from their fangs and goggle-eyed legions of Beelzebub buzzing and skittering brown chitin crunching underfoot and spiny serpents with a hundred delicate legs, crawling, slithering, monsters hidden everywhere. Rats grow plump out there in Uncle Sam's cornfield, where no scarecrow messiah hangs crucified.

The earthen gape swallows his offering with a sprinkle of lime to ease the rot's reek. Secrets are buried in Uncle Sam's cornfield, over eight hundred thousand of them.

Gaze into the Mirror of Belial

Oh you dear poets
Careful of your vanity
Of your hypocrisy
Your phoniness

For we are all phonies
Some more than others
Living our lives under the guise
Of a résumé

Quit empowering yourself
At the expense of honesty

Quit obsessing
Over your number of followers

Oh you dear poets
All your publications
And awards
Avail you not

Who really listens

At the open mics

And who merely waits

For their turn in the spotlight

History will soon forget you

But the universe

Carries your every word and deed

Until the end of time

Betting Against the Fortuneteller

In the future your business suits will be fashioned in militant styles. They'll be more like uniforms, denoting rank and political party affiliation. Your jackets will be made of edible bacon strips, with a tofu option for vegetarians, and your slacks will have built-in folding chairs. Pockets will become obsolete as physical currency gets phased out and your iPhone grows smarter than your iBrain and is installed inside your head. Everyone'll be wearing inflatable undershorts in expectation of the flood to come and wash them all away. Your shoes will have solar-powered lights that turn on automatically when times get dark, and trust me, times will get dark, especially after the EMPs. Pitch as a moonless night in the countryside. Your socks will be bulletproof and weigh a hundred pounds each. You'll wear blinders at work, and your hats will be lined with tinfoil to protect what's left of your soggy brains from mind-control rays. Your neckties will double as nooses for when you finally get it through your thick skulls there's nowhere left to run or hide.

Ode to Big Business

And the men who hold high places
Must be the ones who start
To mold a new reality
Closer to the heart
—Rush (lyrics from "Closer to the Heart")

Are you fine with killing

Your neighbors

Your descendants

Yourself

Death is a joke

To you

Until it's your turn

To be the punchline

Over 90,000 fathers, mothers, sons and daughters

Die from asbestos-related illnesses each year

The Bayer Corporation knowingly sold
HIV-infected blood transfusion products
Throughout Asia and South America

Dupont in my blood
Monsanto in my genes
Nestlé steals my water
While I counterstrike with memes

We can't get rid of the mercury
In our oceans
We can't get rid of the carbon monoxide
In our air
We can't get rid of the plastic
In our soul

"Just a little poison, what could it hurt?" said every
corporation ever.

The entire population of Flint, Michigan
Was exposed to highly toxic amounts of lead
In their tap water

For more than a year

The death toll for the
Union Carbide factory gas leak
Has reached well over 15,000

Smallpox in their blankets
Tuskegee in their veins
Inequality in their workplace
Injustice for their pains

Lynching the past
Enslaving the future
Cutting down family trees
To make room for another shopping mall

We can't get rid of the Walmarts
In our neighborhoods
We can't get rid of the Microsoft
In our words
We can't get rid of the Starbucks
In our soul

"Just a little poison, what could it hurt?" said every
consumer ever.

We are Exxon blood and Chevron lungs
Leadened brains and bellyfuls of glyphosate
Slowly dissolving into Fukushima seas
Under Chernobyl skies

Our flesh and bones
Are made of McDonald's
Polluted with Hollywood hearts
And Maytag minds

"Don't hate the mirror for your reflection," said every
comedian ever.

Mediatizing us with Circus Maximus 90210 24/7
Grooming us for time travel back to the Dark Ages
Cloned sheep herded and fleeced
By monstrous blasphemies
Of ancient gods

Like skillful politicians
They have ten scripted answers
To every yes or no question
None of which
Are yes or no

They blindfold us
With $100 bills
And pour legalistic glue
In our ears

They bite off our tongue
If we speak out
And use it to wipe their ass clean
Of all responsibility

Oil in their bloodlines
Gold clotting up their brains
The extinction of humanity
For monetary gains

"Don't hate the mirror for your reflection," said every
prophet ever.

There's not enough space for everyone
You say
Yet you're big as a skyscraper

There's not enough food for everyone
You say
Yet you consume entire forests

There's not enough clean water for everyone
You say
Yet you drink lakes and rivers dry

There's not enough air for everyone
You say
Yet you inhale ozone and exhale smog

There's not enough love for everyone
You say
With your knee pressing down on our neck

Over 120,000 workers died building the Suez Canal. Over 30,000 workers died building the Panama Canal. Over 100,000 workers died building the Siam-Burma Railway. Over 1,000 workers died building the Transcontinental Railroad. The worst mining accident in Chinese history killed 1,549 workers. The worst mining accident in European history killed 1,099 workers. The worst mining accident in Japanese history killed 687 workers. The worst mining accident in African history killed 437 workers. The worst mining accident in American history killed 362 workers. The worst mining accident in

J. Martin Strangeweather was one of the chief architects of the Tower of Babel. He currently resides in the outskirts of Pandemonium, and can often be found rolling high-grade stones with Sisyphus or trying to outdrink Silenus in foamy black pints of River Styx and golden shots of Lethe. If you've enjoyed any of the writings in this diabolical collection, please donate $1 to the next homeless soul you see.

www.ingramcontent.com/pod-product-compliance
Lightning Source LLC
Chambersburg PA
CBHW030829060726
47590CB00004B/1463